Beatniks and Beehives

The Swinging Sixties

Written and illustrated by
BOB DEWAR

BIRLINN

First published in 2012 by
Birlinn Limited
West Newington House
10 Newington Road
Edinburgh
EH9 1QS

www.birlinn.co.uk

978 1 78027 013 5

British Library Cataloguing-in-Publication Data
A catalogue record for this book is available on
request from the British Library

Designed by James Hutcheson

Printed and bound by
Gutenberg Press, Malta

Contents

Introduction   7

The Era Begins   9

Style and Fashion   21

Leisure Pursuits   33

The Sixties Soundtrack   51

The World of Work   63

Holidays and Travel   73

The Sexual Revolution   81

From Habitat to Hippy Communes   93

Introduction

THE BEATLES, the Stones, Jimi Hendrix, Janis Joplin, the Kinks and Bob Dylan provided the soundtrack to the Sixties, but music was only one aspect that defined the twentieth century's hippest decade. Sex and drugs, as well as rock'n'roll, played their parts too. Mary Whitehouse might have ranted against the evils of the permissive society, but few listened as they groped and fondled their way through the decade towards 1967's great Summer of Love, and no self-respecting hippy commune would be complete without a miasma of marijuana smoke hovering over it.

Looking back, it's easy to get the impression there was a gong sounding 'All Change' on 31 December 1959. But it wasn't as simple as that. The Zen- and Sartre-loving Beat generation, for example, stayed cool well into the Sixties, whilst Teddy Boys continued to brandish flick combs (and flick knives) during the early years of the new decade. Rockers roared into the Sixties on their BSA motorcycles, their arch-rivals the Mods preferring a more sedate mode of transport in the form of a Vespa or Lambretta.

In the world of fashion, the fusty styles of the Fifties gave way to flares, kipper ties, kaftans and Mary Quant. Our daily lives were enriched by visits to Habitat, the freezer centre and Biba (those not in walking distance of Kensington could of course order by mail – as hundreds of thousands of people did), and our homes were transformed with acres of formica and hardboard, G-plan furniture, hostess trolleys and duvets. Prawn cocktail and coq au vin appeared on many dinner tables throughout the land.

Leisure activities too changed beyond recognition. At the end of the Fifties cinema-goers were sitting through films like *Room at the Top* and *Look Back in Anger*, but within a year or two frenzied crowds were flocking to see *Dr No* and *Lawrence of Arabia*. Those

who preferred to stay at home could watch a plethora of new TV programmes, from *The Avengers* to *Steptoe and Son* and *Call My Bluff* to *Top of the Pops*.

People became more adventurous in their holiday destinations too, with many eschewing the traditional holiday camp for a fortnight on the Costa Brava and even more exotic locations. Hippies headed off in all directions of the compass, though enlightenment in the East was the goal of most, and Britain itself became a Mecca for Antipodean travellers, who congregated in Earls Court (aka Kangaroo Valley) in their old VW camper vans.

So much changed during the decade that many have asked the obvious questions: why did it all happen and what caused it? Lots of answers have been offered – society became more affluent, which in turn led to the questioning of the old order, and so on. But this isn't the place to ruminate on such issues – *Beatniks and Beehives* is very much a light-hearted, personal homage. I hope it stirs fond memories of those who lived through the era, and appeals to those who weren't lucky enough to be alive during one of the most exciting decades of recent history.

BOB DEWAR

HEY, LIKE PEACE, MAN

The Era Begins
*Hurrah for Flashy Triviality
and Mass Culture*

The Beats were existentialist, nihilistic followers of Sartre who listened to jazz, protested on behalf of CND, followed Zen (the Way) and were given to sprouting goatee beards and spouting haikus. They were also early believers in sexual liberation – after all, the Bomb might go off at any moment. Euphoric reciprocal conversation of an intellectual nature (usually stressing the futility of life) was the very dab for the Beats too. Anti-style, their uniform was black polo necks, dung-coloured duffle coats with an occasional flash of chukka boot now and again.

Buddha was big stuff with the Beats. Born in Nepal in 563 BC, Buddha (or Siddhartha Gautama as he was at that point) sat under the Bodhi tree and experienced Enlightenment – the search for Nirvana through meditation. All Beatniks studied the Dharma. For some, this was the usual group bonding thingy. Others did achieve a state of oneness with everything – inner calm and flow – Proust and Luke Skywalker would have approved.

Teddy Boys – whose decade of glory was really the 1950s, but who carried on regardless into the early Sixties – wore draped jackets ('drapes'), drainpipe trousers, brothel-creepers and bootlace ties. The coiffure was important. The Tony Curtis or 'DA' (Duck's Arse) involved hair being swept back at the sides and folded in at the back, with an extended, crimped and rolled cowlick at the front. Thick hair gel like Brilliantine kept this tonsorial treat in position. Exhaustive combing with a flick comb was a full-time occupation, though occasionally this was paused to enable whistling and passing comment on passing talent.

Not all Teds were just colourful poseurs, however. Open razors, flick knives and bike chains were essential accessories for some, as were razor blades sewn into jacket lapels. The razor-blades cut the hands of any would-be lapel grabber, allowing the Ted time to assume the position for a quick Glasgow kiss. This kind of Ted would be scary even if dressed in baggy pantaloons and fluffy baffies – perhaps more so, come to think of it.

Unlike the Teddy Boys, Mods and Rockers were true products of the 1960s. Mods were certainly viewed as a bit precious by most Rockers – there can't be much more effete than wearing a big floppy tent-sized parka whilst zipping along on your Lambretta. But they had their own daft moments too, like burning a Morris Oxford or an old Hillman Minx in the street.

Mod Girls – non-committal and wan of face, and generally a lot older than they looked – would strike a kerbside pose until a spare pillion appeared. The elfin urchin look was modelled on Queen of Mods Cathy McGowan (without the smile). The strict Mod look took a dive around '66/'67.

The secret back street barber was known only to local Mods, who would patiently shuffle about outside, shooting their cuffs and inspecting each other's Windsor-knotted ties. This was THE barber – the only one who came up to snuff. Mods would mill about for a couple of hours waiting for their trim – all part of the ritual.

Marlon Brando in *The Wild One* (1954), the underground movie *Scorpio Rising* (1965) and *Easy Rider* (1969) were all an influence on the Rocker culture (though not Marianne Faithfull in *Girl on a Motorcycle*, which was thought not to be up to snuff.)

Rockers were really the younger brothers and sisters of the Ted generation. Also known as Greasers (though oddly enough many had no motorbike), they were attracted by power-dressing and could power slump and glower with the best. But in essence they were nice boys really, who went home for their tea.

The Rockers would roar off to rough-and-ready greasy-spoon caffs, near industrial estates or lorry-drivers' roadside dives, leaving the coffee bars to those of a more Beat persuasion (who were pacifists all). But if they did by chance end up at the same place, there could be some awkward counter-culture clash.

Venerable royal and ancient rockers still cruise the roads today, on their customized 1969 Honda CB750 or the like. These two are members of the Weekend Rogue Relics chapter out for a pudding supper, with ZZ Top clone at the helm.

Style and Fashion
Miniskirts, kipper ties and Mary Quant

Emerging from the 1950s into
the Sixties – when The
Quarrymen played The Cavern
– a lot of kids dressed like their
parents. Boys would wear tweed
jacket and flannels with a nice
crease, whilst young ladies
would sport a sensible hairstyle,
flesh-coloured stockings and a
royal handbag. But this was all
about to change.

Before long boutiques had sprung up everywhere, with their brightly-coloured façades and music belting out from every open doorway. It was all too exciting for words; everybody was having a good time – not forgetting manufacturers of paper carrier bags.

Paper Union Jack carrier bags were an essential part of any fashionable gathering – any self-respecting dolly-bird (genus *Avis Avis Puella Juvenile*) strolling along the King's Road or Carnaby Street would have carried one. This was not a sudden outbreak of nationalism – just part of the original 'Cool Britannia'.

The beehive hairstyle – a towering confection made possible by the application of industrial quantities of spray lacquer – was almost compulsory for many girls in the early Sixties. The then-unheard-of ozone layer must have taken a massive hit. Beehive knocking – tapping on a beehive to test its solidity or wind-proof properties – sounded like someone banging on a door.

There was a firm belief that inside the seldom-washed, frequently-sprayed solidified beehive was a large insect – the lacquer bug – which might chew a hole in your head if angered. Despite this, however, most thought it was worth the risk.

IT'S A WEE BIT OF A WORRY

Flares were often created by sewing inserts into a straight-leg jeans giving a bell-bottom look. The next step was to sew on patches – flowers, hearts, butterflies etc. – covering as much material as possible, or until the sewing became a bore. Trousers with a flare from the knee down were classed as loon pants. 'Loon foot' was when you couldn't see the shoes at all. Splendid.

For the gents, one of the sartorial events of the Sixties was advent of the kipper tie, an item of extraordinary width and eye-catching splendour. The wearer felt it brightened up the faded cardy and battered breeks. This trooping of the colours could probably be seen from the moon.

KIRKINTILLOCH BUGLE

WHERE DO YOU THINK YOU ARE GOING DRESSED LIKE THAT?

SCREAM

The revolution in fashion belonged to the young, despite the embarrassing uncool mothers and other oldish plump folk who adopted plastic hotpants, pedal pushers and miniskirts as their own. 'Please don't drink any vodka; please don't dance; please don't sit down suddenly on the plastic inflatable furniture; please DON'T GO OUT OF THE HOUSE!'

Mary Quant was the patron saint of Sixties style – miniskirts and tights in strong matt colours, big handbags (held like a targe), berets, flat pump ballet shoes an overall geometric style was the look.

Some hung on to a sense of decorum by their fingertips as upmarket women's magazines reflected the new social apartheid with political articles, film reviews, adverts for mail order from Biba and fashion shots of very young, very thin ladies in scrap metal yards and dog tracks. Not much about knitting or the royals – this was all a bit scary. The whole word was clearly out of control and slipping towards oblivion: phone the townswomen's guilds; organize a march; do SOMETHING!

THIS IS NOT A PROPER WOMANS MAGAZINE. WHO IS MARY QUANT? WHAT IS A TWIGGY? BRING BACK GODFREY WINN

Left-wing youth of the Sixties felt no red-brick hall of residence or student flat was complete without a huge poster of Che Guevara (some even knew who he was). Other, more arty, types favoured Aubrey Beardsley, usually the posters for Oscar Wilde's *Salome* (1893) or the *Yellow Book*. These were often printed on sturdy brown wrapping paper. Measurably cool.

Leisure Pursuits
The Hoi Polloi at Play

Friday night was the fave heavy date night. The boyfriend's pay packet was still fairly intact, after paying his parents for board and lodgings. Girls would rush for the bus home, wolf down some egg and chips, change, and spray the beehive before dashing for the bus down town to wait under the clock. The boyfriends chewed polo mints and brushed fag ash from their trousers – gentlemen all – except for those who did not turn up . . .

Hell hath no fury like the stood-up. Ashen faced, livid and hysteric, their theatrical histrionics bordered on violence. Yet they always came back, next Friday.

The posh French restaurant was *à la mode* for the *jeunesse dorée* (and others) of the time. Explore the wine list on the Hotel Splendide Brasserie – perhaps some Blue Nun, Liebfraumilch or Mateus Rosé in its distinctive flask-shaped bottle. But not before an aperitif – perhaps a Martini, sweet sherry or Dubonnet.

Those from the upper echelons of society who spent their youth cloistered in boarding schools felt disenfranchised by the revolutions going on in the outside world. Moral soundness, integrity, probity and obligation were clearly cobblers. Not so cool to be young and posh, yah?

For those not incarcerated in educational establishments, you could just get down and enjoy things … 'Let's twist again, like we did last summer', sang Olympic -standard twistmeister Chubby Checker (who wasn't actually very chubby). First kicked off in Manhattan's Peppermint Lounge in 1961, and helped along by the Beatles 'Twist and Shout' (1963), Chubby sent the short-lived dance craze into orbit everywhere. Other dance crazes included the Frug, the Mashed Potato, the Locomotion and the Watusi.

After an energetic Saturday night, many would spend Sunday evenings under the candlewick bedspread listening to Radio Luxembourg's Top Twenty, interspersed with Horace Batchelor's infra-draw football pools-winning formula, with its address carefully (and slowly) spelled out – K-E-Y-N-S-H-A-M.

Pirate radio stations flourished in the Sixties. Radio Caroline – a former Danish ferry moored three miles off Felixstowe – began broadcasting in 1964, launching the careers of Simon Dee, Dave Lee Travis, Johnnie Walker and Emperor Rosko. When shut down in 1967 under the Marine Broadcastings Offences Act, the station had 40 million listeners. Enter BBC Radio 1, launched 7 a.m. on 30 September 1967, with DJs Tony Blackburn, John Peel, Dave Cash, Kenny Everett, Simon Dee and Tommy Vance.

Those with TVs could also keep up with music on *Top of the Pops*, first broadcast on 1 January 1964, hosted by Jimmy Savile and Alan Freeman, with disc girl Samantha Juste. Whilst there was the added bonus of seeing as well as hearing your favourite bands, many were perhaps more taken with the leggy antics of the Go-Jos, and, later on in the decade, Pan's People, who performed to recordings when artists couldn't be there in person.

The Sixties was one of cinema's golden decades, from *Dr No*, *Psycho* and *Lolita* to *A Fistful of Dollars*, *Lawrence of Arabia* and *Barbarella*. Going to the cinema was a real event – the National Anthem was played over the sound system when the lights came on at the end. Most cinema-goers stood smartly to attention in a creepy Pavlovian way; some even sang the words. Others just slouched, clutching a mass of coats, hats and bags, rolling their eyes and sighing, trapped in the middle of a row by more royalist audience members. A few, sensible enough to have had the foresight to choose an aisle seat, made a run for the exit.

The ice-cream lady sold Orange Maid and Mivvi ice lollies, as well cartons of dubious-tasting orange juice, popcorn and tubs of ice cream. Despite having to endure *ad nauseam* the Pearl & Dean screen adverts, she got to see all the classic films of the Sixties.

Before foreign films went mainstream, small privately owned cinemas showed films like Fellini's *Eight and a Half* or Antonioni's *La Notte*. In contrast to more mainstream venues, film buffs often had coffee served up in china cups and saucers by the usherette. Such cinemas were well hidden in obscure side streets and known only to recherché connoisseurs with a detailed map.

Film connoisseurs were generally thought to be hoity-toity, but many thought they probably only went to see the mucky bits (like the famous nude romp in *Blow-Up*). Fancy preferring that to *Dr Finlay's Casebook*, *Dixon of Dock Green* or *Opportunity Knocks* on the telly?

Lady Chatterley's Lover, the book *célèbre* of the decade, was first published 1928 but banned until 1960. Connie, wife of mine owner Sir Clifford of Wragby Hall, and their gamekeeper, Mellors, were the wanton couple in the hut in the woods. Nothing like an obscenity trial to boost sales – 200,000 sold in one day, it's said!

Long before book towns like Hay-on-Wye and Wigtown, most places had small bookshops everywhere. Many carried a book around with them to confirm their social and intellectual identity – as if that wasn't obvious already. Still you might meet a new chum in the coffee bar or on the bus.

Wifeswapping, along with gardening and golf, was popular in the Sixties. Those who rushed to marry in the late Fifties and settled down in bungalow-land felt a little cheated of the new sexual freedoms enjoyed by the Bolshie youth they saw on the telly. This hobby was never called husband-swapping – so there goes any notion of gender equality.

A more sedate form of entertainment was the Sunday run – not with Nike trainers and bottle of isotonic juice – but off in the Mini somewhere scenic to enjoy the view. Once arrived, out came the thermos, salmon paste sarnies and Sunday papers. The Sunday run had its own strict etiquette – keep the windows shut, don't rustle the papers, don't chew loudly, don't gulp the tea, don't feed the birds, don't feed the sheep (they slobber on the paintwork). Don't snore.

Spearheading all this cultural change was the illegal use of marijuana, grass, ganja, hash, weed, pot, spliffs, reefers, joints and bhang, not to mention stronger stuff. The psycho-active delta-9 tetrahydrocannabinol (THC or just cannabis) was popular with students (all happy wasters), those nasty young rock and rollers, Beats and, allegedly, US Navy personnel. Cannabis use was first recorded in 2700 BC by Chinese Emperor Shen Nong. Warning! Trips can go down as well as up – who would want to come face to face with a bug in a kipper tie!

The Sixties Soundtrack
From Rock Mania to Gritty Blues

Nothing changed as much in the Sixties
as music, but innovations didn't entirely
eclipse the old, so jazz fans – slightly
dazed but delighted – found that rock
hadn't quite taken over the world. Miles
Davis, Dizzy Gillespie, Gerry Mulligan,
Django Reinhardt, Thelonius Monk,
Charlie Parker, Lester Young, Lee Konitz,
Dave Brubek, Art Blakey, Billie Holiday
were all eagerly snapped up. It was like
Paddy's Market.

SOUND PROOF LISTENING BOOTH

Carmen

The sound-proof listening booth in the record store. The peg-board lined glass-fronted booth was good for a free listen to the latest Beatles 45 rpm – share the headphones, come back next week to buy it. Others tried out the classics. Bizet's *Carmen*, a delirium of castanets, whores and murder can't be bad; maybe the 101 Strings' *Soul of Spain* might be worth a go too.

A spontaneous and uncontrollable frenzy – Beatlemania – would break out wherever the decade's most successful band were seen, but the appearance of any *wunderkind* rock star – a Kink, a Stone, a Who – necessitated the services of the St John's Ambulance Brigade. These dedicated and kindly souls carted off hordes of fainters, screamers and vomiters, not to mention the tearful, the white and shakin', the catatonic and the psychosomatic.

ENVIRONMENTAL
DETERMINISM
GROUP BONDING
EXPRESSED AS
STRESS RELATED
CROWD HYSTERIA
LEADING TO EXTREME
PERSONALITY
DISTURBANCE
COMPETITIVE SCREAMS
DERIVED FROM
REPRESSED
BIOLOGICAL URGES

A NICE CUP OF TEA AND
YOU'LL BE GRAND

I'M NO EXPERT.
MIND

VOODOO CHILE

The living room radiogram got a big surprise with the rock revolution. Jimi Hendrix's *Electric Ladyland* was sometimes displayed, and sold too, in a brown paper bag – the ladies on the record sleeve, being naked, were thought indelicate and improper, and likely to offend. But to many of the older generation, so was the music!

Marketed as dangerous, and
with Mick Jagger's East End
accent, strutting and leering, the
Rolling Stones made the Beatles
seem very nice-boy-next-door
types. This suited both bands,
probably.

Eric Clapton – genius guitar man. 'Clapton
is God' was common graffiti on walls from
Land's End to John o'Groats (though the
statement itself was never actually proved).

Rod Stewart – passionate Scotland supporter. Started off with Long John Baldry, then went on to join Steampacket, Jeff Beck Group and Faces, before going solo in 1969 with *An Old Raincoat Won't Let You Down.*

Janis Joplin, known for waving a bottle of whisky around on stage and cursing a lot, as well as general hell-raising – was a fantastic success at Monterey pop festival. Her powerful, big bawdy voice, screams and throaty roar were unique.

If one man summed up Sixties music, it must be Bob Dylan. Born Duluth, on the edge of Lake Superior, Dylan was influenced by Woody Guthrie and Robert Johnson, King of the Delta Blues. But he quickly found his own voice and was signed to Columbia records. Truths – political and social – wrapped in metaphysical verse and accompanied by a guitar and sharp-edged wailing harmonica is one of the quintessential sounds of the decade.

SAD EYED LADY OF THE LOWLANDS

SUBTERRANEAN HOMESICK BLUES

WENT TO SEE THE GYPSY

SEVEN CURSES

LEOPARD SKIN PILL-BOX HAT

IT'S ALRIGHT MA

VISIONS OF JOHANNA

ALL ALONG THE WATCHTOWER

BOOTS OF SPANISH LEATHER

ONLY A PAWN IN THEIR GAME

DESOLATION ROW

FAREWELL ANGELINA

At the other extreme were the folkies, whose music was less political, more basic anthropology, really. Folk singers round the pubs got basic and bawdy and sang about Hairy Mary and Maggie's Old Red Flannel Drawers. An oversized Arran jumper, Breton fishermen's cap and cowboy boots established solidarity with the working man.

The World of Work
All Aboard the Gravy Train

BALL BEARING
POLISHERS MATE

SUPERFICIAL STULTIFYING
PLENTY OVERTIME - FINE

EM

The Employment Exchange. This was an optimistic place – there were plenty of jobs to go around. Stand in the queue for a few minutes, and after a whirl of the rolodex you would come out with a job. Don't be fussy, mind! Nobody thought they wouldn't get a job.

JOINED THE UNION YET-
GOOD LAD
NOW AWAY AND ASK
BIG FERGIE FOR A
LONG STAND AND A
SKYHOOK- THEN GET
A HAIRCUT

There were plenty of apprenticeships too, and the unions were strong. School leavers were contracted as articled trainees, becoming journeymen after suffering what seemed like an eternity of deadpan, sardonic comments from the old hands and double-entendre remarks from the girls in the office.

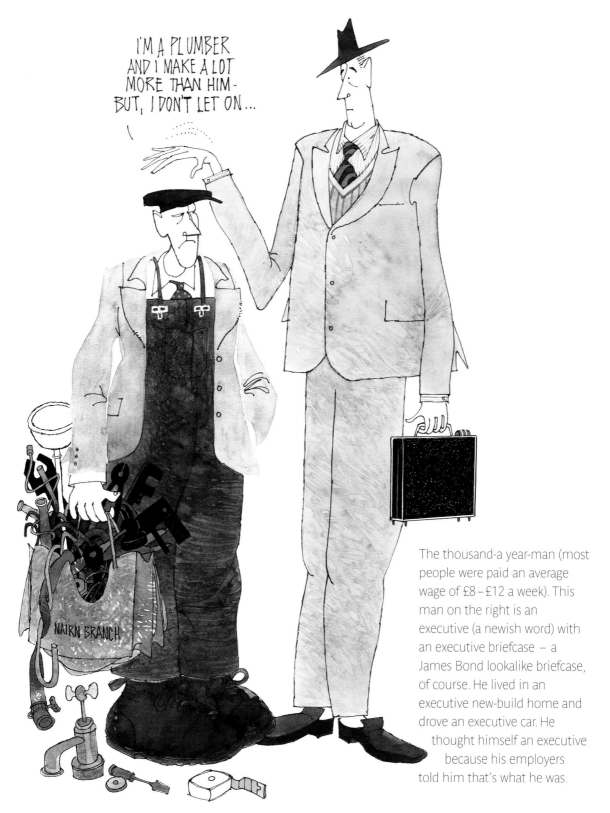

I'M A PLUMBER
AND I MAKE A LOT
MORE THAN HIM -
BUT, I DON'T LET ON...

NAIRN BRANCH

The thousand-a year-man (most people were paid an average wage of £8–£12 a week). This man on the right is an executive (a newish word) with an executive briefcase – a James Bond lookalike briefcase, of course. He lived in an executive new-build home and drove an executive car. He thought himself an executive because his employers told him that's what he was.

A short-hand typist was traditionally recommended as 'a good job for a girl'; typing skills generally eluded the male employees. Men not important enough to have their own secretaries had to make use of the typing pool – a room full of girls battering away on Olivettis, eating Tunnocks Teacakes and engaging in lewd conversations.

In contrast to today, smoking in the office was not a heinous crime. In fact you could smoke almost anywhere: in the cinema, in restaurants and upstairs on the bus. There was little advice about the dangers of smoking.

Even doctors strode the hospital wards with a packet of cigarettes poking out of their jacket pocket.

The pay packet. The brown paper wage envelopes with real pound notes and a few coins were distributed each week round the office by the girl from accounts, there to suffer smart-Alec remarks and amatory innuendo. This ritual would be followed by a thunder of feet – a stampede along the corridor to the Senior Service cigarette machine.

The High Street banks in small towns were friendly and even chummy places (though not open at weekends and closed from three in the afternoon), with ready access to the manager, who placated you with reassuring words about your temporary financial bad spell, the local fete, Dave's sore leg, etc. The staff knew all their customers by name – it was very likely that bank employees had been at school with them. The furniture looked like it had been raised from the Titanic, and the safe was a mighty ex-War Department job. You imagined your small savings deposit growing safely there in the dark – most reassuring.

In the Sixties many people paid £1 a week rent for their council house (these houses were not yet for sale). To buy a house, banks, building societies, estate agents and mortgage brokers would tumble over each other to attract customers. Nice wee homes for £5000. 'How could you lose?' they said. House prices would continue to rise forever. Everyone knew that . . .

Holidays and Travel
The Great Abroad

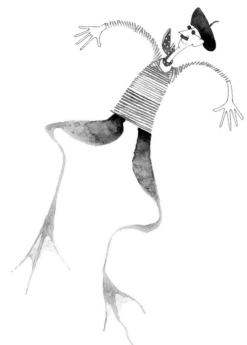

Whilst many continued to enjoy a 'traditional' type of holiday at a holiday camp or boarding house, others were more adventurous and headed off further afield to the Great Abroad. The bravest went off to the continent by car, with a boot full of 'proper food' – packet tea, Nescafé, tins of beans, sliced white bread and Angel Delight. The French lived on frogs' legs and snails soaked in heavy oil; that was a known fact, so best avoided.

Safely off the ferry from Dover, the journey continued down a *route secondaire*. Once the tent was pitched conveniently in a lay-by, out came the camera. Frenzied posing and snapping the signposts followed (this was very important – proving you had been there). Many lay-by campers would be moved on by a gendarme to the nearest official campsite . . .

. . . where cultural differences were highlighted by there being no lavvy pan in the ladies and gents communal toilette. What a topsy-turvy place the Great Abroad was!

After a relaxing fortnight it was only a gentle drive back up the route secondaire to Calais . . .

THIS WAS OUR WAITER HIS NAME WAS AL - AL ADENTE - I THINK HE SAID ...

Once home, slide projectors came out and the lives of friends, family and neighbours were enriched.

The intellectual classes – like academics and writers – had long holidays and sabbaticals. Many hung out in Tuscany, generally avoiding each other. Back home, however, they were more sociable, happy to share their experiences with like-minded colleagues, though whether anyone was listening or not was another matter. Chiantishire was born.

Unlike academics, hippies didn't have holidays, they *travelled*. Whilst thousands went on the hippie trail to the east – Thailand, Goa, Benares and Nepal – South America was popular too. But wherever you went you had to start somewhere . . .

BUS

JOPPA

JEALOUS

HOME TO PUT THE TATTIES ON

TOKYO TRIESTE GOA MEXICO ARTIC LA PAZ BOLIVIA INDIA PEACE USA MOROCCO COSTA RICA

KANGAROO VALLEY

Viva Espanyah...

The less adventurous could always opt for the Spanish package holiday in Torremolinos. Oh, the joy of it all! A week of sun, sea, sangria and Spanish tummy. The return flight always seemed fuller than the outward trip, possibly due to the enormous number of raffia donkeys.

SPAIN

EMBRA

Some, thanks to the Youth Hostel Association, took to the high peaks with Kendal Mint Cake, Yo-yos, thumbsticks, water bottle, compass, map and emergency flares (not the trousered kind). The hostel offered separate beds (male and female dorms) for the night, but not much else. Chores were handed out and you had to make your own breakfast. This was not a type of holiday favoured by the cool and streetwise – 'The Northern Lights of Old Aberdeen' being played on the mouth organ over and over by someone on the back doorstep of the hostel not being regarded as the height of hip.

The Sexual Revolution
Free Pills – and Free Love

Of all the revolutions that took the Sixties by storm, the Sexual Revolution is the one that defines the decade. The contraceptive pill was introduced in 1961 and usually prescribed by the family GP. The Brook Clinics of 1964 changed all that. Before then values were all very traditional . . .

Despite the obvious advantages of the pill, it could still be difficult to find a place conducive to intimacy. Even after a strenuous hike into the countryside wearing winkle-pickers, privacy could not be guaranteed. Being seen *in flagrante delicto* might not upset the livestock, but they certainly didn't approve.

The back two rows of any film house was a heavy-petter's paradise. Missing most of *Psycho* or *Spartacus* was a small price to pay for some slap and tickle. By popular demand some cinemas introduced two-person 'chummy-seats' (don't ask . . .). However, heavy breathing, laughter and other noises related to smooching were not tolerated, and culprits were dealt with severely by the management.

By the Summer of Love in 1967, the repressive moral climate was old hat: sexual freedom was the order of the day. Some took things to extremes, even becoming a little predatory . . .

IMMATURE
FIXATION WITH EROTICA
FILTH AND DIRT - STOPPIT

For many, Mary Whitehouse
was a bastion against moral
degeneracy as she ticked off
the nation and railed against
obscenity, swearing on TV (and
everywhere else, really), in her
Clean Up Britain campaign.
This seemed to go on for years.

Many people didn't take much notice, though . . .

Despite the best-laid plans of dedicated armies of Women's Libbers, Doris Lessing and Angela Carter, many men still referred to 'the wife' or the 'little woman'. They were the breadwinner and wives shouldn't work. OK, there were some women in the office, but they were in the typing pool and just whispered and giggled and knew nothing about golf. A proper wife should stay at home and look after the house.

BEATNIKS AND BEEHIVES

On the other hand a husband seen out in broad daylight with the children would be heavily and loudly disparaged by the local Mafia of matriarchs. To compound this infamy, should the children be wearing incorrectly coloured clothing (blue for a girl, pink for a boy), thus deliberately flouting a key precept of Darwinian evolution, contemptuous abuse would escalate to extraordinary levels.

Any husband shopping on his own for a bag of Kerr's Pinks without close supervision would be fair game for chorus of tutting and sighing from expert female shoppers. It might be speculated that he even hung out the washing – almost unthinkable – if so his virility would be seriously brought into question.

VENOMOUS HISS – DIDJEESEE THAT – A WEE GIRL DRESSED IN BLUE! NOT PROPER.

Fathers were not welcome to attend the birth of their baby. Any who tried would be met by an NHS bouncer, who would bar the doorway to the maternity unit, exercising her absolute powers of refusal. To have a husband in at the delivery, with his accompanying hysteria and fainting, would not have been tolerated.

From Habitat to
Hippy Communes
. . . and Things To Do
with Hammers and
Hardboard

The lives of many changed as people searched for new self-definitions. Professor Ossowski's book *Class Structure in the Social Consciousness* suggests that legislation affecting incomes, housing etc. caused massive change in society. The new homeowner became the home improver, and DIY was born. Sheets of hardboard and shiny Formica were the clean lines of the new age.

The flush-panelled fireplace was almost compulsory for the Sixties DIY improver, as picturesque tiles were hammered out and the surround stripped away to the brickwork. All this was done to prepare for the *pièce de résistance* – an electric fire with plastic coal and red light bulb to give that warm, cosy feel.

Barry Bucknell's step-by-step
home improvement TV shows,
Barry Bucknell's Do It Yourself
and *Bucknell's House*, were
hugely popular. The nation was
gripped by flush-panel fever –
doors with hand-crafted, carved
panels were suddenly the
height of bad taste and quickly
covered by hardboard sheets
to give that sleek, modern look.

Things were changing in the kitchen too, of course. As part of the culinary fever inspired by Elizabeth David's bestselling *French Provincial Cooking* and *French Country Cooking*, many a suburban house boasted a French farmhouse kitchen. Enter the Aga, a big scrubbed pine table (what better to serve hare in cream with chestnut purée on?), ethnic pottery, Sabatier knives and a load of other *batterie de cuisine* from Habitat.

Any epicurean housewife would source her fresh fruit and veg at local markets. This was an exhaustive process which involved critical, close scrutiny and pummelling of fruit and vegetables (you couldn't get away with this at the Co-op) before they were bought and deposited in the ubiquitous wicker basket.

Others embraced the new technology of the home freezer, filling it to the brim with ready chopped frozen veg from the echoing halls of the freezer centre. This was shopping for a new, hectic lifestyle.

The revolution in serving food was epitomized by the serving hatch – that two-foot square space that allowed a seamless flow between kitchen and dining room. Lots of new-build council houses had serving hatches – something that made many people feel they were definitely on the way up.

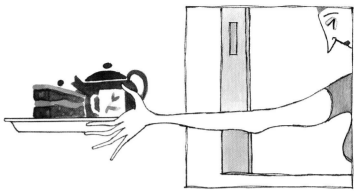

Many middle-class housewives aspired to the hostess trolley, a device which meant the lady of the house didn't miss out on the fun and could enjoy without stress the usual dinner party fare – Ruskolene-coated Chicken Kiev with ready-chopped carrots, processed peas and some tinned potatoes, all nicely tepid. (The prawn cocktail starter and black forest gateau with cream pudding didn't require the trolley treatment for obvious reasons.) Dinner parties were a breeze, and some Blue Nun or Chianti Ruffino would ease any sticky moments. Chicken Maryland and lemon cheesecake at the neighbours' next week . .

Freedom from washday drudgery was the promise to proud owners of the twin-tub washing machine. Attach the inlet and outlet rubber hoses to tap and sink and away you go. However, a secure knowledge of man-made fibres – acrilan, terylene, nylon, courtelle, dicel, tricel, spanzelle – and a sound understanding of stain removers – carbon tetrachloride for chewing gum, turpentine or lard for paint, and oxalic acid for rust – was still required. There was also sorting, soaking, boiling, starching, drying and ironing. It was still a busy life for those escapees from washday drudgery.

Formica – the easy-wipe heat-resistant surface – seemed to stretch to the horizon. It was used everywhere, for everything, from kitchens, frothy coffee caffs and lavatories to kitchen cabinets and tea trays. Raspberry pink and primrose yellow were the favoured colours.

Terence Conran's Habitat shops, which started in swinging Chelsea in 1964, with their Mediterranean pottery and Japanese-inspired paper lantern shades saw off any vestige of frumpy Fifties interior design. Much admired by the new kids on the block, who would load up their VW Beetle or Citroën with futons and pasta storage jars.

The duvet rang the death knell for the slippery nylon quilt, and put an end to tedious blanket-tucking. The continental quilt – duvet or downie – had snuck in from France, Germany and Nordic lands. Kapok or down-filled, this was a must for hip young homemakers.

The G-Plan chair was an icon of the Sixties. It tilted, rocked and swivelled – what more could you want? Perhaps the egg chair; the high-tech Charles Eames, metal-piping and leather chair; the bean bag? All these were cool, except perhaps the bean bag, but the G-plan was king of them all. Was it a G-plan chair Ernst Stavro Blofeld sat in stroking his cat in *You Only Live Twice* …?

Of course many turned their backs on the empty symbols of capitalist lifestyle and returned to nature, by way of sustainable drainage, Shaker-style furniture, hens, tepees and herb gardens – all essential components of the hippy commune.

Self-sufficiency was the aim of any self-respecting commune-dweller, but until that could be achieved, bulk-buying of life's essentials – macrobiotic goodies, lentils, brown rice, rizlas and toilet rolls – was *de rigueur*.

As in many tribal societies, women did most of the work . . .

LENTILS